PARÈS SCALES

For Individual Study
and Like-Instrument Class Instruction

by GABRIEL PARÈS

Revised and Edited by Harvey S. Whistler

Published for:

Flute or Piccolo . . . . Parès-Whistler

Clarinet . . . . Parès-Whistler

Oboe . . . . Parès-Whistler

Bassoon . . . . Parès-Whistler

● Saxophone . . . . Parès-Whistler

Cornet, Trumpet or Baritone 𝄞 . . . . Parès-Whistler

French Horn, E♭ Alto or Mellophone . . . . Parès-Whistler

Trombone or Baritone 𝄢 . . . . Parès-Whistler

E♭ Bass (Tuba - Sousaphone) . . . . Parès-Whistler

BB♭ Bass (Tuba - Sousaphone) . . . . Parès-Whistler

Marimba, Xylophone or Vibes . . . . Parès-Whistler-Jolliff

For Individual Study and Like-Instrument Class Instruction
(Not Playable by Bands or by Mixed-Instruments)

RUBANK, INC.

HAL • LEONARD®
CORPORATION
7777 W. BLUEMOUND RD. P.O. BOX 13819 MILWAUKEE, WI 53213

Key of C Major
Long Tones to Strengthen Lips

Scale of C

Also practice holding each tone for EIGHT counts.
When playing long tones, practice (1) ⟨ and (2) ⟨⟩.

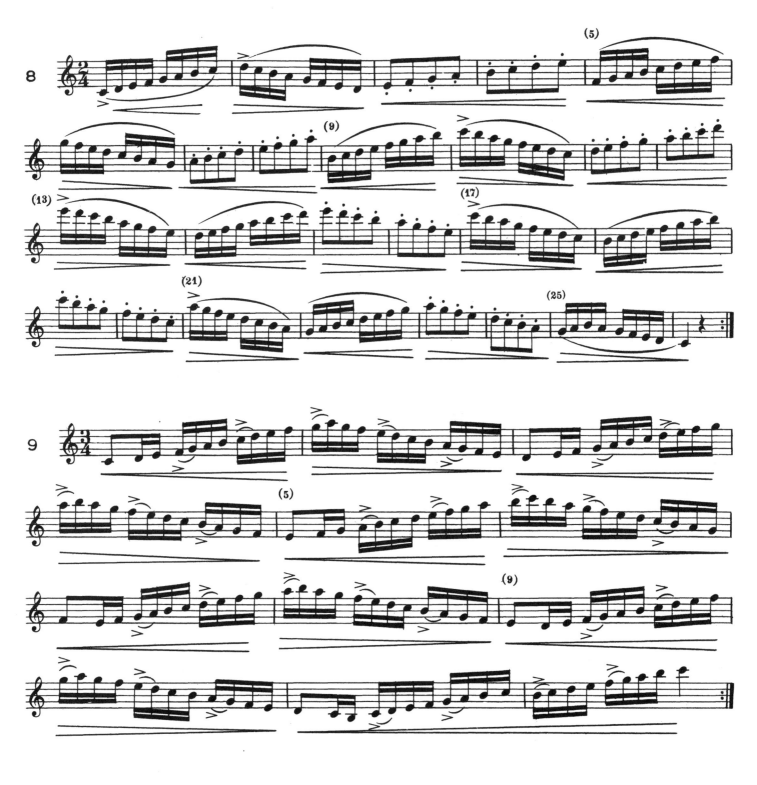

Embouchure Studies

Slur as many tones as possible

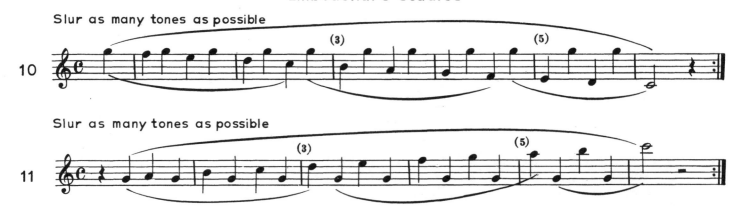

Key of G Major
Long Tones to Strengthen Lips

12 Scale of G

Also practice holding each tone for EIGHT counts.
When playing long tones, practice (1) ‿ and (2) ‿ ‿.

13

14

15

Embouchure Studies

Slur as many tones as possible

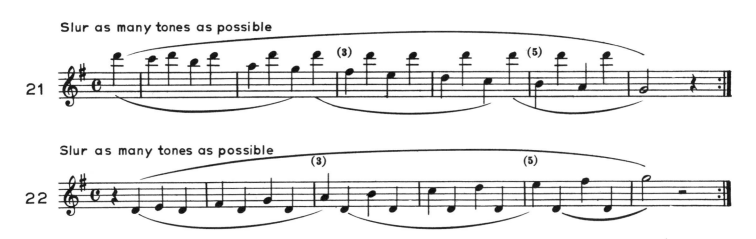

Slur as many tones as possible

Key of F Major
Long Tones to Strengthen Lips

Scale of F

23

Also practice holding each tone for EIGHT counts.
When playing long tones, practice (1) ⟨ and (2) ⟨ ⟩.

Embouchure Studies

Slur as many tones as possible

Slur as many tones as possible

Key of D Major
Long Tones to Strengthen Lips

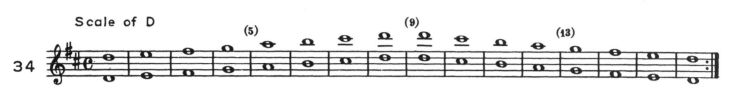

Scale of D

34

Also practice holding each tone for EIGHT counts.
When playing long tones, practice (1) ⟨ and (2) ⟨⟩.

35

36

37

Embouchure Studies

Slur as many tones as possible

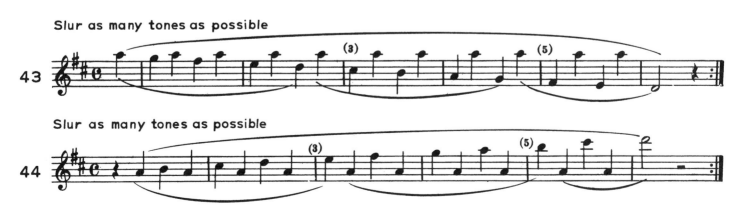

Key of B♭ Major
Long Tones to Strengthen Lips

Scale of B♭

45

Also practice holding each tone for EIGHT counts.
When playing long tones, practice (1) ⟨ and (2) ⟨⟩.

46

47

48

Embouchure Studies

Slur as many tones as possible

Slur as many tones as possible

Key of A Major
Long Tones to Strengthen Lips

Scale of A

56

Also practice holding each tone for EIGHT counts.
When playing long tones, practice (1) ⟨ and (2) ⟨ ⟩.

57

58

Embouchure Studies

Slur as many tones as possible

Slur as many tones as possible

Key of E♭ Major
Long Tones to Strengthen Lips

Scale of E♭

66

Also practice holding each tone for EIGHT counts.
When playing long tones, practice (1) ⟨ and (2) ⟨⟩.

Embouchure Studies

Slur as many tones as possible

Slur as many tones as possible

Key of E Major
Long Tones to Strengthen Lips

77

Also practice holding each tone for EIGHT counts.
When playing long tones, practice (1) ⏦ and (2) ⏦⏦.

78

79

80

Embouchure Studies

Slur as many tones as possible

Slur as many tones as possible

Key of A♭ Major
Long Tones to Strengthen Lips

Scale of A♭

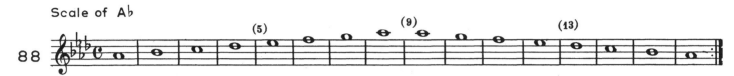

88

Also practice holding each tone for EIGHT counts.
When playing long tones, practice (1) ⟨ and (2) ⟨ ⟩.

Embouchure Studies

Slur as many tones as possible

Slur as many tones as possible

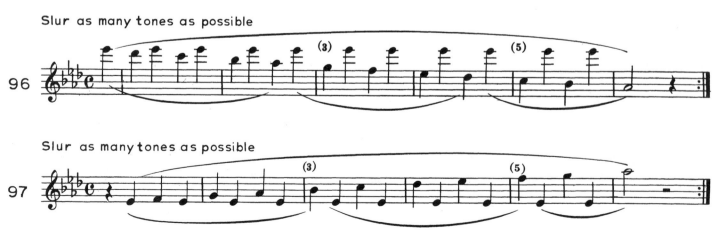

Key of A Minor
(Relative to the Key of C Major)
Long Tones to Strengthen Lips

Scale of A Harmonic Minor

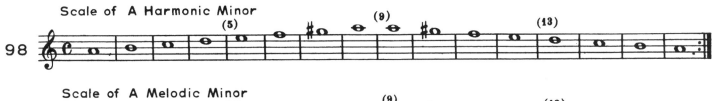

98

Scale of A Melodic Minor

99

Also practice holding each tone for EIGHT counts.
When playing long tones, practice (1) ⊂ and (2) ◁.

100

101

Embouchure Studies

Slur as many tones as possible

102

Slur as many tones as possible

103

Key of E Minor

(Relative to the Key of G Major)

Long Tones to Strengthen Lips

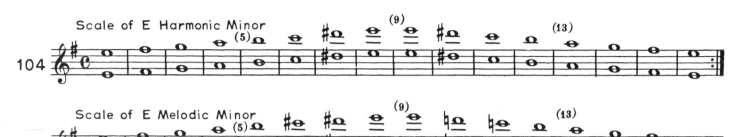

Scale of E Harmonic Minor

104

Scale of E Melodic Minor

105

Also practice holding each tone for EIGHT counts.
When playing long tones, practice (1) ⟨ and (2) ⟨⟩.

106

107

Embouchure Studies

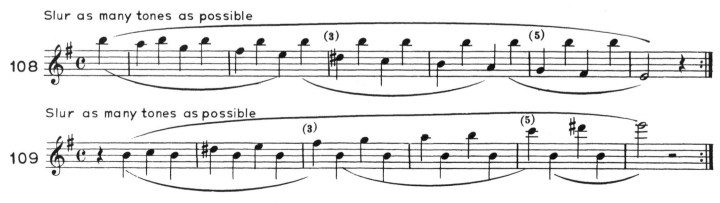

Slur as many tones as possible

108

Slur as many tones as possible

109

Key of D Minor
(Relative to the Key of F Major)
Long Tones to Strengthen Lips

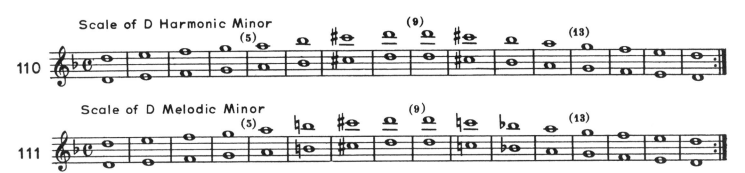

Scale of D Harmonic Minor

Scale of D Melodic Minor

Also practice holding each tone for EIGHT counts.
When playing long tones, practice (1) ⟨ and (2) ⟨ ⟩.

Embouchure Studies

Slur as many tones as possible

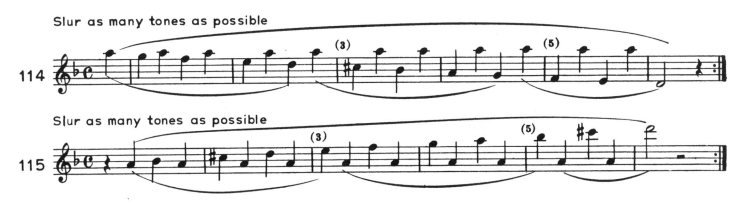

Slur as many tones as possible

Key of B Minor
(Relative to the Key of D Major)
Long Tones to Strengthen Lips

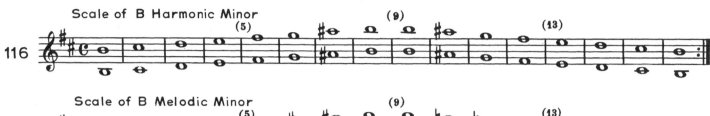

116 Scale of B Harmonic Minor

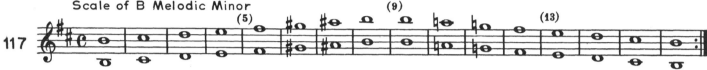

117 Scale of B Melodic Minor

Also practice holding each tone for EIGHT counts.
When playing long tones, practice (1) < and (2) <>.

118

119

Embouchure Studies

Slur as many tones as possible

120

Slur as many tones as possible

121

Key of G Minor
(Relative to the Key of B♭ Major)
Long Tones to Strengthen Lips

Scale of G Harmonic Minor

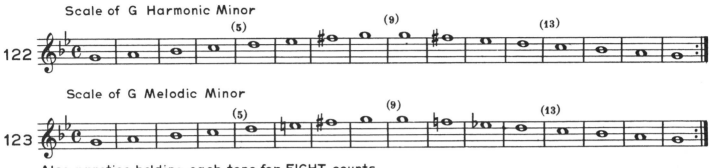

Scale of G Melodic Minor

Also practice holding each tone for EIGHT counts.
When playing long tones, practice (1) ⟨ and (2) ⟨ ⟩.

Embouchure Studies

Slur as many tones as possible

Slur as many tones as possible

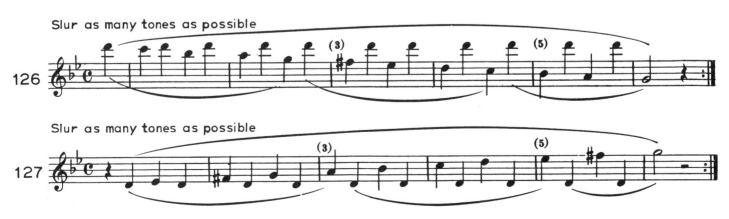

Key of F# Minor
(Relative to the Key of A Major)
Long Tones to Strengthen Lips

Scale of F# Harmonic Minor

128

Scale of F# Melodic Minor

129

Also practice holding each tone for EIGHT counts.
When playing long tones, practice (1) ⎯⎯ and (2) ⎯⎯⎯ .

130

131

Embouchure Studies

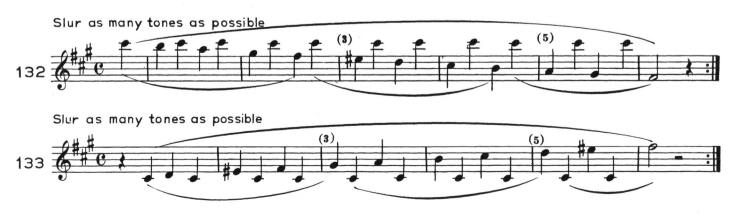

Slur as many tones as possible

132

Slur as many tones as possible

133

Key of C Minor
(Relative to the Key of E♭ Major)
Long Tones to Strengthen Lips

Scale of C Harmonic Minor

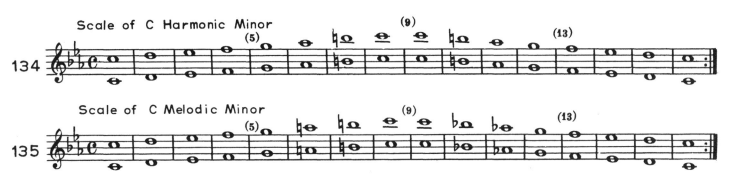

Also practice holding each tone for EIGHT counts.
When playing long tones, practice (1) $\diagup$ and (2) $\diagup\diagdown$.

Embouchure Studies

Slur as many tones as possible

Slur as many tones as possible

Key of C# Minor
(Relative to the Key of E Major)
Long Tones to Strengthen Lips

Scale of C# Harmonic Minor

Scale of C# Melodic Minor

Also practice holding each tone for EIGHT counts.
When playing long tones, practice (1) $\diamondsuit$ and (2) $\diamondsuit$.

Embouchure Studies

Slur as many tones as possible

Slur as many tones as possible

Key of F Minor
(Relative to the Key of A♭ Major)
Long Tones to Strengthen Lips

146 — Scale of F Harmonic Minor

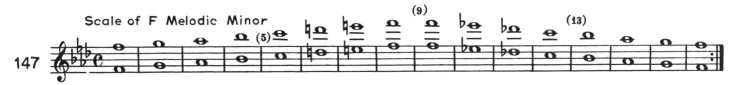

147 — Scale of F Melodic Minor

Also practice holding each tone for EIGHT counts.
When playing long tones, practice (1) < and (2) <>.

148

149

Embouchure Studies

Slur as many tones as possible

150

Slur as many tones as possible

151

Major Scales

Harmonic Minor Scales

Melodic Minor Scales

Arpeggios

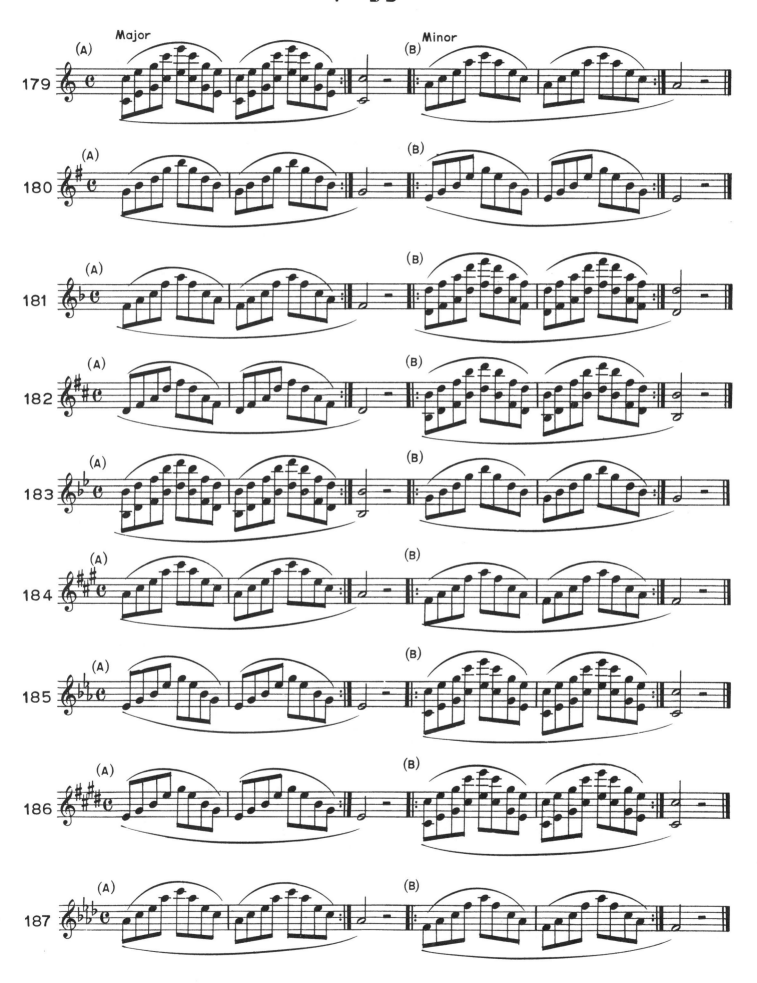

Chromatic Scales

Chromatic Scales in Triplets

Two Octave Chromatic Scales

Two Octave Chromatic Scales in Triplets

Basic Exercises to Strengthen Low Tones

Also practice holding each tone of each slur for (1) FOUR counts, and (2) EIGHT counts.

Also practice TONGUING each tone of each slur.

Basic Exercises to Strengthen High Tones

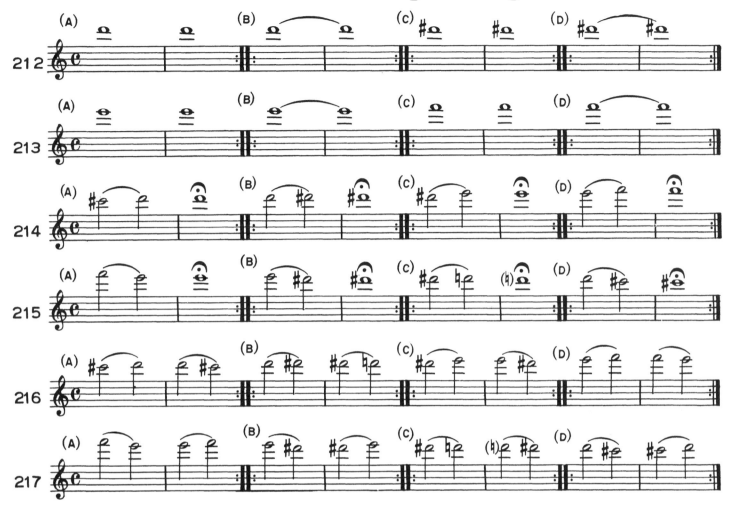

Short Studies in the High Register

(a) Also practice very slowly, holding each tone for (1) FOUR counts, and (2) EIGHT counts.
When playing long tones, practice (1) ⟨ and (2) ⟨⟩ .

(b) Also practice very legato, (1) slurring each two tones, and (2) slurring each four tones.

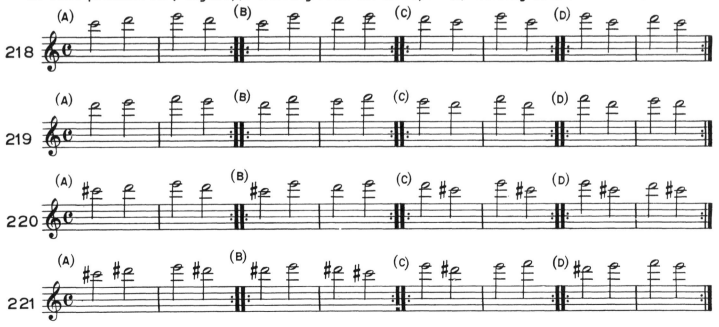

Studies in Mechanism

Scales in Thirds

Exercise in Sixths

Combined Thirds and Sixths

Octave Study